Historical Research in Archives

A Practical Guide

By Samuel J. Redman

ABOUT THE AUTHOR: Samuel J. Redman is an Assistant Professor at University of Massachusetts at Amherst. He received his BA in anthropology and history from the University of Minnesota, Morris and his PhD in U.S. history from the University of California, Berkeley. In the course of his research, he has worked in over 20 archives, including the Regional Oral History Office (ROHO) of the Bancroft Library at the University of California, Berkeley, where he was an academic specialist.

AHA EDITORS: Robert B. Townsend and Pillarisetti Sudhir

LAYOUT AND COVER DESIGN: Christian A. Hale

© 2013 by the American Historical Association

ISBN: 978-0-87229-202-4

Published in 2013 by the American Historical Association. As publisher, the American Historical Association does not adopt official views on any field of history and does not necessarily agree or disagree with the views expressed in this book.

LIBRARY OF CONGRESS CATALOGING-IN-PUBLICATION DATA:

Redman, Samuel J.

Historical research in archives : a practical guide / by Samuel J. Redman.
pages cm

Includes bibliographical references.

ISBN 978-0-87229-202-4

1. History—Archival resources—United States—Handbooks, manuals, etc. 2. History—Research—Methodology—Handbooks, manuals, etc. 3. Archival materials—United States—Handbooks, manuals, etc. I. Title.

D16.R329 2013   026'.9072073—dc23   2013017484

CONTENTS

ACKNOWLEDGMENTS

At the University of California, Berkeley, I have been blessed with an outstanding circle of mentors and friends. My advisers—Richard Cándida Smith, Randolph Starn, and Thomas Biolsi—have guided me immensely in learning to develop the craft of historical research. I have benefited immensely from conversations with historians at other institutions, including a recent conversation with Steven Conn at Ohio State University. At Berkeley, several of my fellow graduate students were especially helpful in organizing ideas for this pamphlet. I wish to thank Phillip Wolgin, Dylan Esson, Tim Ruckle, and Jacqui Shine in particular. Ira Jacknis shares my love of anthropology and history, and we productively shared many ideas about the same archives.

Most of all, I owe a debt of gratitude to the many archivists who helped me collect ideas for this volume. The idea for this pamphlet came about during my year at the National Anthropological Archives, Smithsonian Institution. There, I was given numerous suggestions and shared many delightful and enlightening conversations with an absolutely outstanding collection of archivists. Especially helpful were Leanda Gahegan, Daisy Njoku, Gina Rappaport, and Lorain Wang. Jennifer Snyder at the Archives of American Art and Michael Pahn at the National Museum of the American Indian also contributed to my thinking about archives in innumerable ways. I would also like to thank Alessandro Pezzati, University Museum Archives, University of Pennsylvania. Lastly, conversations with friends and colleagues at the Bancroft and Doe Libraries helped clarify certain ideas. This included especially David Farrell and David Kessler, who are both extremely generous with their time. Any mistakes or errors of judgment in this pamphlet, however, are entirely my own.

1. INTRODUCTION

For researchers unfamiliar with the process of working in archives, the challenge of completing a project requiring study of primary sources can be daunting. For new researchers and for those embarking on a new project, reading existing scholarship and organizing research questions into a coherent research proposal is often the easy part. For many, the real challenge begins when they enter the archives and begin collecting, organizing, and analyzing primary source materials.

Historians can be a somewhat reticent bunch when discussing specific details of their approach to work in the archives. While we frequently discuss our methodological and theoretical approaches to the *writing* of history, we rarely talk about the best approaches to our work in the archives. When I was starting work on my undergraduate thesis, my advisers offered little coaching on how to work in the archives to collect and then deal with research material. This allowed me the space to design my own approach to my collections of sources; but considerable time was taken up by trial-and-error efforts. By the time I enrolled in graduate school, I had a fair amount of archival experience, though I began work on my dissertation without ever having received formal training on how to approach archival research. At first, I was embarrassed by this fact and kept it to myself. But eventually, I started to discuss the lack of training in archival research with other historians and learned that most in the field receive little guidance on how to conduct archival research. We learn the methodological and theoretical approaches to *reading* primary sources, and we learn how to craft these sources into historical writing. But we are rarely coached on how to *find* these same sources in the archives or how to deal with them once we find them.

This pamphlet works to address this educational gap by offering some basic advice on how to go about working in archives in the 21st century. Consider this guide a starting point, rather than an encyclopedic resource on conducting historical research in archives. Although this manual is derived mainly from the author's experiences in numerous archives in the United States and uses examples drawn from U.S. archives, much of the guidance offered here can be used by those working in archives in other countries as well. Searching for archival materials, organizing notes, and planning a research trip are just a few of the many topics explored in this pamphlet, which is intended to help researchers embarking on projects in the archives.

This pamphlet seeks to help such researchers by introducing some contemporary approaches to working in archives in the United States: from tracking down possible archival sources to the nuts-and-bolts of recording information. It also offers tips for organizing archival material and for utilizing new technologies in the archives. This volume is intended for all kinds of historical researchers—beginners who have never been inside an archive, seasoned professional historians, or amateur historians conducting genealogical research. New historians will find the entire pamphlet useful, while more seasoned researchers may find it useful for refining their own practices—perhaps by further developing the new approaches to archival work discussed in these pages.

Instead of offering only a few precepts that researchers can implement directly, this pamphlet offers *ideas* for working in modern archives. Not all of these ideas will be applicable to every source; nor will they suit every individual. But they can serve as entry points for historians to reflect on their craft.[1] This volume contains several sections organized into the many stages of a typical research trip, starting with the preparations for an archival visit before even stepping away from your desk. Most archives in the United States provide information online about their collections and this information can prepare you to ask targeted questions or requests to an archivist. Well-crafted and detailed questions based on your preliminary research online can save both you and the archive's staff time. Subsequent sections continue with the theme of preparation and offer a few suggestions for setting realistic goals based on what you learn on the web and over the phone.

Continuing the practical advice on preparing for a research trip, the next section offers a guide to new technologies in archives. Visit any major archive in the United States and you will see historians working with laptops, cameras, scanners, and tablets, but nearly every archive has its own set of rules about these new technologies. Further, simply because a new technology is available, that does not mean it will be useful for your research. This section will attempt to address some of the pros and cons of various new technologies for your research.

The sections that follow offer several suggestions for building relationships with archivists and other historical researchers during your time in the archives. Building positive and productive relationships with archivists should, in fact, be a vital part of your daily life in the archives, as these relationships often produce direct benefits, both in your immediate research and in your subsequent career. In addition to professional etiquette, this section also suggests a few ways in which historical researchers can also help archivists and archives.

The final two sections of this pamphlet offer suggestions on basic methodology. They examine potential problems with restricted collections, lost or missing materials, and collections which appear to be of use in the finding aid yet are of little value upon actual viewing. As part of this, I will offer several suggestions for taking notes and organizing your research materials. Many of these ideas are not new, but this section should help the reader either develop or build on existing note-taking methods. This section also offers tips on how to organize the new kinds of materials technology helps the historian collect—including digital photographs and scans.

The examples described in this pamphlet represent an amalgam of experiences and observations from my archival research as well as conversations with numerous historians and archivists.

2. SCOPING OUT THE ARCHIVES

New technologies and materials found on the Internet are fundamentally changing the nature of historical research. Search engines and research databases are providing historical researchers with a vast array of published primary sources. In providing access to millions of sources, the web allows historical researchers to garner a general understanding of a particular body of historical material before even venturing into an archive. Unfortunately, while many archives in the United States have begun to digitize sources to make them available online, the overwhelming amount and variety of archival material available in most repositories makes the complete digitization of archival material practically impossible. In addition to the massive number of documents, digitization requires a number of conservation considerations. Unlike the "quick and dirty" process of scanning your recent family photos into a computer, the staff of an archive has the responsibility to handle historical documents with the care necessary for irreplaceable artifacts. Whereas many wire services and major newspapers have digitized their archives, for instance, local newspapers are often only available as original copies or on microfilm. Historical researchers, therefore, must often leave the comfort of their home libraries to study collections available only at archival repositories.

Before leaving on a research trip, however, scholars should take the time to fully explore the web sites of all relevant archives. Doing so will provide a general understanding of the archives and the way it organizes its materials, which helps fine tune research requests and makes the job of the archivist and researcher that much easier. Although the search tools provided on an archive's web site may facilitate an exhaustive search, recall that not all materials available in the archive are likely to be listed in online catalogs or finding aids. You should be prepared to describe to an archivist what materials you have found online, and what kinds of sources you are hoping to find when you ultimately visit. Since historians tend to be concerned with individuals and institutions, origins, and events, archives try to maintain records pertaining to things like institutional origins and major events.[2] Searching an online catalog and the web site of an archive should usually come before sending an archive an e-mail or calling on the phone.

The first step in scoping out archival sources online is to select a series of themes, keywords, and names that summarize your research. Bear in mind that records are often arranged by name, geographical location, period, or by number. These keywords will eventually help you narrow down particular collections, but they also help you identify which archives will likely contain documents of relevance to you. Archives in the United States range from the massive collections of the federal government (such as the National Archives), to smaller archives of local historical societies (for example, the Goodhue County History Center in Red Wing, Minnesota), and to thematic collections (such as the National Gay & Lesbian Archives in Los Angeles, California). Similarly, if your research requires the use of rare published volumes not available at your home institution, knowledge of finding aids and library catalogs will likely help you explore special or rare book libraries, such as the Medical Historical Library at Yale University.

Carefully organizing the early stages of your research will help you bring a massive archive, such as the National Archives, down to a more manageable scale. A research project on the subject of atomic weapons research, for instance, will likely begin with secondary research. A simple trip to the library will provide the names of important politicians, social activists, government programs, and legislative acts related to the topic. Starting at the National Archives web site (www.archives.gov), a search for the phrase "Manhattan Project," for instance, reveals several relevant collections. From there, one can click on several specialized collections based on particular individuals, legislative acts, themes, or relevant periods. It is important to keep track of groups of records that you find of interest. When creating a new research project, I typically create a new folder on my computer and then create a series of word documents to organize particular collections within the larger folder. These files will help me keep track of the actual documents I view later on in the process.

Continuing with the example of the Manhattan Project, the National Archives' web site lists several collections related to the secret project to create an atomic weapon. One such collection is listed as, "Press Releases Related to the Atomic Bomb and Atomic Energy, compiled 1945–1946." If I click on this collection, a new page gives me important information about the group. The collection happens to be housed in the National Archives facility in College Park, Maryland, and falls under a larger Record Group for the Department of the Navy. These types of web pages, found through searches on an online database, typically provide brief descriptions of the collection and explain how the material has been organized. The web page may also provide a link to the finding aid for the collection.

If the finding aid is available for online perusal as well as downloading, be sure to download a copy to your computer in order to carefully search the document and have on hand for subsequent reference. This information—starting with the URL of the web sites you examine, the name of the record group, and the numbers of the particular boxes that appear to be of interest—should all be recorded carefully. Listing call numbers, box numbers, specific names of collections, record groups, or control numbers can all assist an archive in helping you find the physical boxes represented virtually in an online database.

Smaller archives, like their larger, often better-resourced counterparts, have started to place basic information about their archive and their finding aids online. Unfortunately, many archives have neither the time nor funds to place all of their catalogs or finding aides online. If this is the case, archivists will typically inform you via e-mail that a catalog for a particular collection only exists in hard copy format and can only be consulted in the archive or library itself. Even if the catalog exists digitally, some historians or archivists prefer using a physical copy of a particularly important finding aid (or one that is otherwise not so easy to understand). Archivists will sometimes pull hard copies of finding aids off shelves in order to answer questions because they are often easier to look over with another person than a single computer screen. You may learn about the availability of these collections from secondary sources or word of mouth. Alternatively, you might simply make an educated guess as to what might be in a particular archive due to the nature of the institution. Archivists, even if they possess only limited online resources, should be able to help you navigate available collections in person, over e-mail, or on the phone.

Spend time entering your keywords individually into the online catalog or the search function of the archive. Typically, I enter a handful of keywords into a catalog over the course of just a few moments in order to get a better overall grasp of what the archive holds in their collections. Look for names, places, ideas, and keywords associated with your research. Try various combinations of the terms and understand that some online search functions are more effective than others. Pay attention to what kinds of collections are predominant in the archives and ask some basic questions about them: Do the collections that show up in the search results consist mainly of personal or institutional papers? Are the collections held in the archive mainly thematic or are they organized around a particular geographical region? Try to organize your initial keyword searches around the types of collections you expect to find in the archives. Following my initial search, I usually go back and re-enter each phrase more judiciously, recording the citations I find for collections of interest.

When a particular collection relevant to your research is listed in the search results, experiment with the links to see if the hit will lead you to a more expansive finding aid or simply a catalog entry. A small catalog entry—the equivalent of a virtual catalog card—should provide you with enough information to actually start finding material in the archive. Whereas a complete finding aid will likely explain the contents of the entire collection, the search function might only point you to a specific box containing documents relevant to your keywords. Often, the web sites for archives will link to a downloadable copy of the larger finding aid. Once you have a copy of the finding aid, make sure to repeat a search for the relevant keywords, noting the types of documents you are likely to find in each collection. You will notice that the search functions for most web sites will miss certain collections, while turning up unexpected hits in other collections. The key to an exhaustive search is repetition: entering keywords into search functions for the entire archive, repeating them when searching the finding aid, and then scanning for them when you actually view the materials.

Eventually, you will want to search more methodically, recording the exact results of what you have found and what searches were unsuccessful. Some scholars will create a spreadsheet of their various "hits" from a particular archive, others will simply write them down on paper or in a separate document. The collections I tend to work with are organized by the name of the individual or institution that created or gathered them; therefore, I create a separate document for each collection that I examine. While still at home examining a finding aid on my computer, I write down what boxes seem to be relevant to my research within each of these new files. At the top of this new document, I copy and paste in the relevant links and information from the online database, and perhaps also make a few notes on the collection, summarizing what I have discovered in the finding aid. This means that by the time I arrive at the archive, I can simply open the document, and request the appropriate boxes listed in my notes. Later, I can reopen the document and remind myself about the nature of the collection by scanning the first few lines.

Spend some time thinking about how the documents in particular collections are organized. Did the archivist who processed the collection choose to organize materials chronologically, by theme, or by name? Does the organization of materials appear to be true to its original format (called "original order"), or was it rearranged when it was acquired by the archive where it is now housed? Try to understand the methods of the people who organized this material. This will help you to predict the kinds of documents that will be in particular areas of the collection, eventually saving you time as you hone this skill.

A number of web sites, including the *Online Archive of California and American Memory*, serve as virtual directories or clearinghouses, as they link to numerous archives from one single location on the web. Even if you are planning to work eventually with a single archive within the coalition of archives maintaining such a portal or "clearinghouse" site, you should try searching with the group or "federated" search function in addition to using the search engine on the web site of the specific archive. The algorithm that operates each search engine can shift your results and you can turn up different hits on each web site. Additionally, working on web sites that display the collections of multiple archives can reveal unexpected collections in a manner different from searching on the web site of a single archive.

As you begin to record the results of your search, the most important thing you can do to help your own cause is to stay organized [**fig. 1**].

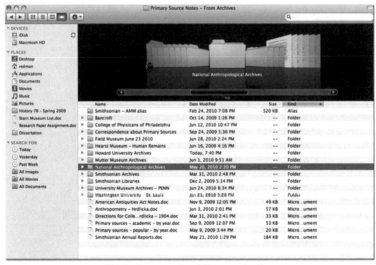

Fig. 1: An example of file organization.

My own organizational system is arranged by archive and collection. Because I have worked in a number of different archives with a diverse array of collections, this has helped me to keep track of where I found particular documents. If you tend to work in one major archive with a smaller number of collections, you might want to organize your materials differently, perhaps around keywords. Numerous software programs allow historians to organize digital files more easily and you should speak to colleagues about what programs they are using whenever possible. No matter how you organize your notes, when you find a result, record what it is you have found and exactly where you have found it. Make sure to err on the side of providing *more* information—list the citation for the archive, collection, and boxes, but also copy a link of the web site into the document or spreadsheet you are using to document your research. Later, if you need to confirm something with the archive, or write to them for additional photocopies, you will want to provide an archivist with as much detailed information about your inquiry as possible. If you are unable to find online finding aids for collections that you are turning up on the web, make sure to contact the archive, describing the relevant finding aids you would like to view. Whenever possible, save copies of digital finding aids for your records. Many archives are still in the process of digitizing online catalogs and sometimes, the finding aid itself is the last item to be fully digitized. Consider noting in your records where the original finding aid or other reference materials related to important archival collections can be found. In my notes, at the very top of the page, underneath the citation for the location of the material, I record my immediate thoughts on the significance of the entire collection for my research. You can adjust these notes as you move forward with the project, but providing yourself with a series of reminders will be useful over time.

3. General Preparation

While preparing this pamphlet, I consulted with a number of other historians. Although I asked different questions of each of the experienced researchers, one of the questions I began every session with was to ask for the single most important piece of advice that they could offer to a new archival researcher. One historian lit up immediately, explaining that the difference between a successful day at the archives and a fruitless day at the archives came down to preparation. If you enter the archives *knowing* what you are looking for, he argued, you are far more likely to be successful and efficient with your time. If you wander into the archives simply hoping that you will find relevant material, you are less likely to find useful sources. Preparing for a visit to the archives can itself be labor intensive and time consuming, but the time you spend organizing materials before the visit will invariably help you to be more efficient once you are actually in the archives. You can also do this work on your own time—on weekends, evenings, or during airplane flights—whereas the archives themselves are only open during standard business hours.

Preparation can make the difference between a researcher arriving at the archive and explaining in overly broad terms: "I'm interested in indigenous accounts of encounters with Europeans," or being helpfully more specific: "I'd like to see your materials on Lakota Winter Counts for my project on indigenous accounts of encounters with Europeans in the mid-19th century." Although the benefits of making research requests in the latter form may be common sense to many, a surprising number of historical researchers arrive at archives without giving the archive's web site and the available online finding aids even a cursory glance. Further, I have watched in amazement as researchers arrive with cameras at archives that do not allow photography, without lunches when food service is not available onsite or nearby, and perhaps worst of all, with little sense of what they are looking for and how the available materials fit into their own projects. In order to avoid these and other simple missteps, take a moment to review the rules and any "frequently asked questions," or "visitors guide" sections available on the web site of the archive where you plan to work. This is an even more important preliminary step if you are planning to work in a foreign archive, far from home. Archives in other countries often have different rules for requesting materials or even for gaining admission, and it is essential that you become aware of these *before* you go.

Your first step in preparing for an archival visit should be to define the scope of your overall project. If you are working on a dissertation, for instance, you should begin by articulating the nature of your project in the form of a dissertation or thesis proposal. This exercise will encourage you to discuss the overall goal of your project, articulate how it fits within the existing scholarship, and define the various components of the project. A book or article on Lakota contacts with Europeans in the 19th century, to utilize the above example, fits within the broader scholarship of borderlands and Native American history in the United States, and you might be visiting an archive to find sources for a chapter exploring how Lakota Winter Counts changed materially throughout the course of the middle of the 19th century. Clearly defining your goals for an archival visit will be a great benefit to your work. It will be useful, for instance, to determine which components of your larger project might be benefited by a particular archival visit. Once you have defined the scope of your project and what you are hoping to find on any given day, finding aids and archivists can help guide you to the appropriate sources. Without a doubt, time you spend in the archives will, in turn, give you a better understanding of the exact nature of your own project, which you are likely to redefine once you begin working with primary sources.

Despite deceptive similarities, archival catalogs that can be consulted online possess several key differences from a library catalog. While library catalogs direct you to discrete volumes of books, archival catalogs generally direct you to more nebulous collections of materials, consisting of a variety of documents in a wide range of sizes. A particular collection might include a single photograph that could take only a few seconds to examine or a series of rooms full of boxes that would take a lifetime to exhaust. While searching online for keywords relevant to your project, bear in mind that archival finding aids simply cannot list every relevant keyword to describe their holdings. A collection of a hundred letters might need thousands of keywords to be accurately and fully described. Researchers should consider wading through larger collections of documents to complete an exhaustive search of a collection while also weighing the time constraints of such an approach. It is worth noting that such deep and extensive searches might sometimes prove extremely disappointing as you might find only duplicates or multiple copies of the same document—because they were preserved in the archives while other documents you hoped to find are not available as they never reached the archives.[3]

Once you have a grasp on the nature of your project and which archives will be important to your research, spend some time familiarizing yourself with the geographic area around the location of the archive. Depending on the nature of your visit, this preparation can mean simply browsing the web site of the archive, or a more intense planning session. In order to prepare for an recent visit to an archive in an unfamiliar city, I spent some time creating maps from my hotel to the archive, briefly looked for a highly rated deli within a block of the facilities, and found the location of a pub suggested by a colleague residing in the same city who met me for dinner at the end of the workday. While these conveniences come second to finding actual sources in the archive, streamlining your visit will allow you to focus on your research during the duration of your visit. Simply put, this sort of preparation also makes your time in the archives more pleasant and will allow you to focus on your research.

The web sites of archives vary widely in their completeness and usefulness. Some archives will provide a list of their rules and protocols, tips for working with their catalogs and finding aids, and offer a few suggestions of where to eat lunch. Other web sites are sparse and will only give you limited information with which to plan your visit.

4. Technology in the Archives

Bringing the right tools to your research visit is another essential part of your preparations. New technological resources, including cameras, scanners, laptops, and tablets are rapidly changing the nature of archival research. Most archives in the United States now allow researchers to take notes on laptops. Over the course of the past few years, many archives have also developed additional policies on the use of cameras and scanners. Archives should, therefore, be contacted well in advance before attempting to utilize any of these devices in a reading room. While these tools generally benefit the researcher, the potential costs and benefits of each technology should be carefully considered when developing your methods for working with archival collections.

New Technology and Methods

When I started working in the archives, even just a few years ago, I recorded my notes using a pencil and a notebook. Since that time, I have shifted my note-taking to a laptop computer. I can record notes on my laptop faster than I can write them out longhand. Even better, these notes are easily searchable. If I am composing a lecture or essay on Teddy Roosevelt, for instance, I can quickly access the lecture notes I have taken from other scholars, my reading notes from secondary sources, and any archival materials authored by the former president that I may have transcribed. With handwritten notes, I would have to recall exactly where these notes were stored and attempt to find them within each notebook.

While technologies often improve the ability to record and organize archival materials, researchers also run the risk of adopting a technology that might soon be outdated. Before embracing a new program or piece of technology, find out if previous versions of those technologies allowed data to be transferred to newer technologies. The benefit of paper notes, of course, is that they are preserved for a lengthy period without having to be transferred to new media. Voice notes recorded on a tape recorder, on the other hand, are obsolete as soon as that particular type of medium becomes an outdated technology. Digital images, documents typed in a basic word processor, and notes organized by basic file folders, however, seem to be fairly stable in terms of changing technologies and these kinds of files can often be easily transferred between Mac and PC or different types of document formats. Hard copies of these documents can also be printed as backup and can be stored in multiple locations. Long range preservation of certain technologies, such as CD-ROMs or DVDs is unknown at this time. Backing up files in as many locations and in as many formats as possible, is a highly recommended practice for all and most certainly for scholars.

Before committing to a large-scale research project with a new technology, consider testing the technology on a smaller archival research project. Test the method on an article, for instance, before using the system for an entire dissertation or book manuscript. When organizing notes and images using new technologies, keep your system as clean and simple as possible. I organize my materials by the name of the archive, then the name of the particular collection. Within my notes on the particular collection, the box number, file name, and description of the document of interest are recorded. Within a few seconds, I can access a particular document and cite where, exactly, that document was originally found in the archives. Digital images or scans affiliated with those collections can be placed into a separate folder within the folder of the archive, and a word processor document noting the exact citation for each photograph can be placed in the folder for the archive as well. Although it is time consuming to write notes detailing the citation for every photograph or scan taken from the archive, you will be happy that you did so if you needed to retrace your steps several months later. Just as with your citations for an eventual publication, your organizational system should allow you to retrace your own steps several months or years in the future.

CAMERAS

Digital cameras are increasingly becoming common as tools to record archival documents. Although special permission is almost always required for using cameras, the reading rooms of both the largest and smallest archives often contain scholars using cameras to digitize portions of the collections for later reference. Cameras offer several benefits to researchers:

they can create copies that are less expensive than a typical photocopy; they allow you to rapidly copy a collection; and with appropriate light and space, you can easily photograph everything from a small postcard to a large map. I have even used cameras to take photographs of documents on microfilm reading screens, which are often more legible than the poor (and expensive) reproductions obtained from an attached printer.

While cameras can be an important component of the historian's toolkit, they are far from perfect. Many archives still do not permit their use. And at a functional level, memory or battery power often runs out at the least convenient times. As a researcher, you should consider several factors when purchasing a camera. It has become less necessary to worry about resolution or pixels; almost any new camera will have enough megapixel power for photography in the archives. Instead, balance the features against the size and durability of the camera; you will typically need to sacrifice bells and whistles for a camera that is easy to carry and has longer battery life.

Here are a few basic questions to consider.

Are you using this camera solely for professional purposes or for personal reasons as well?

While working in the archives, I use my camera for taking dozens and dozens of photographs of hard to find collections. When at the lake, I use the same camera to document my time with family and friends. These are important things to consider when purchasing a camera. You will find that many high-quality cameras easily allow you to jump between different kinds of lighting and macro or micro settings; some cameras will even have a black-and-white "documents" setting. But you should be sure to ask an expert at an electronics or camera store about the ability of the camera to take photographs in different settings.

Does the camera allow you to easily and clearly disable the flash and audio settings?

Most archives will not allow flash photography either because it disturbs other researchers or because objects and documents can be damaged by the bright flash. When testing a camera, take a few photographs of a book or newspaper under the florescent light of the store with the flash disabled. Does it capture a clear, readable image? Then try turning the camera off and then back on again; does the flash remain disabled?

If yes, this can prevent an embarrassing situation where you have turned the camera off in order to save battery power, only to find that you've turned on the flash when restarting the camera. Many cameras allow you to turn off audio settings (in particular the "shutter" sound of cameras and the noise some cameras make when the device is turned on or buttons are pushed). When purchasing a new camera, check to see if audio can be easily muted for work in the archives.

Does the camera have a document setting or a macro setting?

As a researcher, it is important to consider how the camera will operate when taking photographs of the sources you will likely encounter. For my own research, I most often document standard 8"x11" papers, with standard typewriting or handwriting. A basic modern camera with a decent macro setting (a specialized function for taking pictures of objects that are very close) will almost always capture this material. If you are hoping to document large maps or much smaller objects or documents, however, it would be wise to talk to a specialized camera sales associate/salesperson before investing in a camera.

Does the camera have an image stabilization function?

Many modern cameras also come standard with a function to minimize the distortions caused by vibrations from your hand. While you might be a sure-handed photographer, this function can save you time by allowing you to take photographs at a slightly faster pace without spending extra seconds making sure the camera is set up exactly right each time. It is useful to have a camera that allows you to take photographs without a tripod. A few archives allow cameras, but do not allow tripods. And sometimes you may need to photograph objects of different sizes (a map, documents about a map, and a small tag cataloguing the map, for example).

Will the camera allow you to use a tripod?

The reason for asking this question is perhaps obvious. Holding a camera in the same position for hours can be surprisingly tiring. Additionally, your hands may shake just enough to blur an image taken from the camera, especially when taking photos with the longer exposure required when shooting in low light without a flash. Even if you don't plan on using a tripod right away, you might consider buying a camera that will allow you to use a tripod in the future. Once again, bear in mind that a small number of archives do not allow the use of tripods.

Does the camera have a large viewfinder?

Another factor worth considering when purchasing a camera for historical research is the size of the viewfinder, or the screen on the back of the camera. I do not have the best eyesight, but in my extra large viewfinder I can see if a photograph of a document is legible. When the photograph is blurred, I simply take a duplicate photograph and check the viewfinder for image clarity.

How quickly will the camera "refresh" after taking a photograph?

When taking hundreds of photographs in an archive over the course of a single day, the last thing you want to do is spend time waiting for your camera to process a new image and refresh, allowing you to take another photograph. Even a few seconds can feel like a waste of time if you are taking photos in rapid succession—for instance if you are photographing an entire file for future reference. As you test cameras, get a feel for how quickly the camera refreshes after processing each photograph.

SCANNERS

Photographs certainly allow fast and low-cost recording of documents. but scanners provide historians with a detailed, more accurate image of any particular document.However, scanners can be frustratingly slow and the images they create are often nearly indistinguishable from those captured with a traditional camera. But if you are a historian whose sources regularly require you to carefully examine small handwriting or marginalia, or if you are gathering material for publication online, a scanner might be more useful.

There are several factors to consider when selecting a scanner for archival work: Do the archives where you work allow the use of scanners? Will you use the scanner primarily to record historical documents, or will you be utilizing it for multiple purposes? Is the scanner lightweight and compact enough to transport from location to location? Does the scanner conform to the regulations in place at major archives?

A good list of potential problems can be gleaned from the National Archives and Records Administration's regulations regarding scanning documents in research rooms. Portable handheld scanners, for instance, are not allowed in many archives because they involve physical contact between the scanning mechanism and the original documents to digitize them, potentially damaging the archival material. And scanners that emit a high amount of light or heat are also prohibited at most archives.

If you know which archive you will be conducting the bulk of your research in, be sure to check its web site or call to ask about its particular rules for scanning documents.

LAPTOPS AND TABLETS

The laptop computer is perhaps the main tool of the modern researcher. Most archives allow researchers to take notes on a computer. My laptop is also reasonably light, allows me to compare files quickly, and lets me create new filing systems on the spot, mimicking the archival collections in front of me. I can quickly share files, e-mail questions, correct mistakes I might find in multiple kinds of files, and update my to-do list based on what I accomplish. Although certain kinds of tablet computers can do many of these things, a laptop computer remains the most versatile and useful tool for archival research. In a few years, tablet computers may prove to be more effective tools for archival research. If you are interested in a tablet device, such as the iPad, you should first experiment with one in a store to get a feel for the functionality and note-taking features of the device. Due to the rapid pace of technological innovation, you will have to continually study your options for these kinds of devices. If you are lucky, your employer or school will provide you with a computer, but it is more than likely you will be on your own when purchasing a new computer. This section offers a few considerations to keep in mind when purchasing a laptop for historical research.

WHAT IS THE WEIGHT OF THE LAPTOP? IS IT CONVENIENT TO CARRY?

Just as with cameras, for laptops too, there is usually a trade-off between weight and functionality (not to mention price). Recall that when you conduct archival research, you will likely be traveling to a number of different places. A lighter laptop—which, for a given price, means a smaller screen and less power—makes such travel easier. Most of the time you can do without the extra processing power or the larger display that a heavier laptop normally brings, unless you frequently need to crunch numbers in a spreadsheet or refer to documents and images.

If you are using it just to type and take notes, a smaller laptop or netbook should be sufficient, but test the keyboard to ensure that you feel comfortable using it for long stretches. Tablets are even more portable with the additional advantage of a long battery life between charges, but you may need to use an external keyboard. Tablets with cameras may come in handy for recording images of documents.

WHAT ARE YOU INTENDING TO USE THIS LAPTOP FOR?

Researchers tend to use laptops for multiple uses. We read the newspaper over morning coffee, and then use the same laptop to read secondary literature and work on a manuscript. At my office desk, I have hooked up a larger monitor to my laptop, allowing me to read primary source documents while revising a manuscript at the same time. When purchasing a new laptop, I have to consider whether or not the machine will allow me to multitask in the way to which I have grown accustomed.

CAN YOU EASILY BACK UP IMPORTANT FILES?

Computers can crash or can be stolen; coffee can be spilled all over them at some cafe. Almost any historian you meet can tell a story of regret about files lost due to some catastrophe. Regularly backing up data is, therefore, essential. Newer Apple computers feature a program called Time Machine that allows you to easily backup all of your files onto an external hard drive. PCs can also be attached to external hard drives. A thumb drive or external hard drive, makes it easy to backup all your files. Ensure, in addition, that you have multiple copies of important files in separate locations. New developments in so-called cloud computing can assist historians by allowing them to back up files onto an off-site server.

5. Setting Realistic Goals

As you make the final preparations for your research trip, be sure to set realistic goals for your visit, and allow as much time for research as possible. Several archivists observed that one of the most common mistakes researchers make in the archive is a failure to budget enough time to find and examine primary sources. Constraints of time and resources often force researchers to budget too little time for archival research; to a certain extent, these constraints are unavoidable. But historians can learn to maximize their time in the archive by being selective about the materials they choose to transcribe, scan, or photograph.

While certainly not the norm, two stories might shed some light on possible problems with trying to budget a certain amount of time for an archival trip. In 2008, while working at the National Archives, I planned a very short amount of time to look at a collection of material that was described in a finding aid as "3 linear feet." When the collection finally arrived, I was surprised to see that it filled an entire, large cart. I checked with an archivist who helped me look over the reference, and we eventually realized that a typo in the finding aid listed the collection as "3 linear feet," rather than the accurate size of the collection—300 linear feet. As far as typos go, this one was extreme. Nevertheless, it was a useful reminder to allow time for the unexpected whenever possible.

In addition to potential surprises in the materials, you can also encounter external impediments to research. During a recent visit to an archive, the entire building was forced to evacuate because an armed intruder had entered another part of the building. Thankfully, nobody was harmed. However, the unexpected incident cut short the workday. An archivist lamented to me a few days later that one researcher who had scheduled only one eight-hour workday in the archive was unable to complete his work at the due to the events. This is an extreme case, of course, but veteran researchers can recall many cases where a day of research was lost to weather, illness, or other unexpected circumstances.

The bottom line: when you are traveling to an archive, prepare for the unexpected and budget ample time for your work. On the other hand, what if you budgeted time for a collection of 300 linear feet, and it turns out to be only 3 feet? What if the material described in the finding aid turns out to be totally irrelivent to your project? If you are concerned that you have budgeted too much time for a particular project, spend a few minutes exploring other finding aids in the same archive, taking a moment to consider another collection if you find yourself with spare time. This might also be an opportunity to speak to an archivist about other collections in the archive. I always keep future projects in the back of my mind, transcribing a few notes here and there for future scholarship. If you have the luxury of extra time, why not look at a collection that will be useful for future research? Archival visits can also provide historical researchers with the opportunity to spend time in the surrounding area and your schedule may already include a visit to another nearby repository. While many historians are forced (or feel compelled) to spend every waking second of their research visit either in the archives or in a hotel room writing, you should also try to find balance during your visits to the archives. If you can, take the opportunity to tour nearby historic sites, monuments, and museums. If you are racked with remorse during a research visit because you have budgeted too much time, consider taking photographs of nearby historic sites for future lecture slides.

While I recommended that you be liberal with the amount of time you budget for archival research, other historical researchers will suggest that "less is more." Something that may seem *interesting* in the archives may not actually prove to be significant to your work. Researchers have different methods for addressing this problem. Some historians will start to write up the preliminary results of their study early on in their research, in order to gauge where holes in their narrative might exist. Others will simply try to predict what material will be useful as evidence in support of a possible thesis. Historical researchers should continually ask themselves how the materials they are reading in the archives may or may not relate to their current project. If a particular document seems relevant, take the time to record it. However, if a document merely seems interesting but is only tangentially related to your work, it would be wise to weigh the value of recording the document against the possibility of finding more relevant materials—either in the same collection or in another collection or location.

6. Building Relationships

Working with Archivists

While working at the archive where I completed the bulk of my dissertation research, I had the opportunity to closely observe the interactions between researchers and archivists. The archive had one designated reference archivist, but each of the archival specialists (those who worked primarily with photographs, processing, or audio/visual materials) would take turns covering the reference desk. I was pleased to note that with a few exceptions, most historical researchers put their best foot forward when first meeting archivists, treating them with the dignity and respect that is the ethically proper approach to any professional from whom help is being sought. Not surprisingly, the archivists also responded in the same way, more often than not with similar professional courtesies, and often went beyond the requirements of their duties to be helpful. This section offers some commonsense advice on etiquette in the archives, which, if followed, will make your research easier and more productive.

The archives where I did most of my own dissertation research had a basic set of protocols for researchers. Researchers needed to make appointments beforehand, but they were notified of this fact and could fill out a simple web form alerting the archive of their schedule and desired materials. Upon their arrival at the archives, researchers were required to check in with a security guard at the front desk. After that, an archivist met them and guided them to the reading room. Researchers were then asked to fill out a few brief forms and their materials were promptly brought to them at their desk. Such protocols are fairly common in most archives and straightforward. If you call an archive in advance, or send an e-mail prior to your visit, these sorts of procedures can be explained in 30 seconds or less. Just follow the instructions of security guards and archivists, and you will have your materials at a comfortable work space in under half an hour.

Following instructions and protocols is a necessary and useful step. Building productive relationships with archivists is an equally important step as it accomplishes several things, not the least of which is that the archivists are then more likely to make your research easier and more efficient.

Many archivists are sincerely interested in the research resources that are in their archives and they want to see you succeed in finding materials contributing to your research. This process of collaboration will become considerably easier if you can explain your research goals and describe what you are seeking in the archives in clear, unambiguous terms.

PRACTICE YOUR "ELEVATOR TALK"

When you arrive at an archive, many reference archivists will ask you to describe your research project. All you need to do is to provide the archivist with a few conceise sentences about your work. Ideally, you also want to pass along some of your enthusiasm for the project to the archivist. These conversations serve a practical function, as archives often record how researchers are utilizing their records. This exchange also provides an opportunity right at the start of your visit when archivists can suggest other records that may be relevant to your research, but which you may not have considered. Archivists who "buy-in" to your project will tend to work even harder on your behalf. A long-winded, detailed sales pitch will not be useful for this purpose. What you need is a succinct overview of the research project with clearly stated objectives for that archives. A two- or three-sentence description of your project and further two- to three-sentence descriptions of each chapter or section of your project will be sufficient. You may find it helpful to practice this "elevator talk" about your project, as you may have to repeat it in several archives, and it will save you time while also clearly communicating your research needs. You should also detail what kinds of documents you are hoping to find and attempt to answer any follow up questions the archivist may have with brief, but detailed responses. When an archivist starts asking questions about your project, they are primarily hoping to help you narrow down a collection to a particular set of useful documents, and they might have in mind other archival documents not readily visible from online finding aids. So, unless the archivists specifically ask, it will be unhelpful and counterproductive at this juncture to describe your research methodology or discuss your theoretical framework.

Explain in Basic Terms What You Are Hoping to Find

In addition to explaining the overarching themes of your project, it would be wise to provide archivists with a bit of information about what kinds of sources you are hoping to find. Articulating these details to an experienced reference archivist can help you in a surprising fashion. What follows is a hypothetical example. A historian is hoping to find information about the travels of a particular intellectual who is the primary subject of an ongoing project. Upon arriving at the archive, the historian explains that he is writing an intellectual biography of a particular feminist, and that he has discovered from the finding aid for the collection that both her correspondence and diaries are in the repository. The scholar explains to the archivist in plain language that he has found a gap in the literature and he would like to know whom this historical feminist intellectual met with while traveling through Europe in the 1920s. The archivist might suggest looking through both the diaries and the correspondence, but may also note a third option: the official records of an institution that employed the feminist intellectual in question. With any luck, the archivist suggests, a list of speaking engagements might be found in the annual report of the organization, which was hoping to promote the work of affiliated intellectuals. This is just a hypothetical example, but when working with an experienced archivist, worthwhile suggestions like this are forthcoming all the time, as long as the researcher is willing to explain the project in clear language and is clearly willing to listen to the thoughts of the archivist.

Over the course of my time in archives, I have seen dozens of examples of archivists pointing historians in new directions. Archivists can better help historians if they know the scope of their project and something about what we, as scholars, are hoping to find.

Learn a Bit about Your Archivist

Archivists and librarians are often professionals in the expanding field of information and library science. Graduate and professional programs provide extensive training to individuals hoping to assist scholars with their research. Though not all archivists hold graduate degrees—you will routinely encounter interns or recent graduates with little experience—you also find archivists to be exceptionally well qualified to assist you with your research. A popular and accomplished professor of mine left my undergraduate institution to become an archivist after returning to graduate school in information and library sciences, for example. These individuals should be treated with sincere professional respect. Although it seems like common sense, treat the archivists and staff you encounter with collegiality. These individuals have often spent years organizing the archive and their intimate knowledge of the materials can be supremely useful to your research.

If you are yourself embarking on a career working in the archives, it is worthwhile to take a few moments to think about *why* someone might become an archivist or librarian caring for a special collection. If you have the opportunity, have informal conversations with archivists, perhaps over lunch. Ask what interests them most about the archive and why they decided to get into the profession. You might be introduced to collections useful for your research and teaching—or you might make a new friend or professional contact.

OBSERVE THE "GOLDEN RULE" AND PROFESSIONAL BOUNDARIES

Here is a not-so-dirty secret about archives and archivists. Because they are normal human beings with regular feelings and emotions, they will often go out of their way to assist researchers who are nice to them. At one archive where I spent a considerable amount of time, I observed that the archivists dealt with hundreds of photocopy requests. Researchers who had reputations for being rude, bossy, or snobbish were treated differently from researchers who were friendly, patient, and engaging. Certainly, it is sometimes true that in the short term, the "squeaky wheel gets the grease," but when organizing a queue of documents to photocopy, an archivist can easily bump the photocopies of a friendly individual to the top of the pile. Since most archivists have numerous responsibilities beyond making photocopies, this task will often be passed along to an intern or done when the archivist has time. Simply, if you are professional and friendly, an archivist is far more likely to make time for your copies.

As researchers, the least we can do for our colleagues is to be courteous with individual requests. Come to the archives with an idea of what you are hoping to find and be grateful when an archivist works with you to find other relevant materials. Researchers should remember to send thank-you notes to especially generous archivists, and always cite their contributions in the acknowledgement sections of books and articles.

CONSERVATION OF ARCHIVAL MATERIALS AND HOW TO HELP YOUR ARCHIVE

In addition to demonstrating basic courtesy and respect, there are ways in which you can, as a historical researcher, actually help the archivists in their mission of preserving and sharing historical documents. The first is by recognizing and reporting mistakes in the organization of collections. Historical researchers can also alert archivists to documents in need of attention from conservators. Finally, researchers can also make a note of collections they find unique or interesting to give archivists a better idea of the scope and uniqueness of the collections in their archives.

Never attempt to reorganize documents or folders independently. Instead, approach an archivist when possible and explain what you are seeing. Periodically, you will come across a collection intended to be in a certain order that has been misfiled. If you have a laptop, you can point to the finding aid and show the archivist the mistaken collection and politely ask for permission to fix the order of the documents. The archivists will likely thank you for pointing out the mistake and either offer to take care of it on their own, or allow you to rearrange the material. Be respectful of their decision and thank the archivists for their help.

Although nobody expects you to be an expert in conserving the primary source documents with which you work, the collections you examine for your research should always be handled with great care. The archivists you are working with will provide you with guidelines for handling different types of documents. Glossy photographs, for instance, are typically handled with gloves to avoid transferring the oil on your hands to the original documents. Researchers can also notify archivists when documents are in need of conservation attention. Paper documents that are fraying or falling apart upon handling should be noted or "flagged" with bookmarks provided to you by the archive. These documents will often be placed in a protective sleeve to slow the process of decay. Original metal staples or paperclips, which can rust, are sometimes replaced with archive friendly plastic paperclips (or removed altogether), to prevent further damage to the document. Researchers can also keep an eye out for bugs (either living or dead) and anything that appears to be unusually dirty in archival material or special collections. Pests can be a major problem for archives—they can eat the original documents during their lifetime, and their carcasses can provide food for other possibly damaging pests. Typically, an archivist will examine the documents that are noted to be in need of attention and take the appropriate next step. Since archivists rarely examine entire collections first-hand, recognizing potential conservation problems with collections can greatly help an archive.

Historical researchers can also help archives by pointing out interesting or unique collections to the archivists responsible for them. Remember that some archivists will know particular collections like the back of their hand. They may often work with researchers on that particular collection, or they may have played a role in acquiring or processing that particular collection. Nevertheless, it is likely that your research—reading the relevant secondary literature, comparing various archival collections, and constructing a historical narrative—will allow you to note particular collections or documents of value that might build the institutional knowledge of the archive staff. Without coming off as aloof or pedantic, simply try to be engaged and helpful when discussing a collection with an archivist.

MEETING OTHER HISTORIANS

Spending time in an archive sometimes offers you the opportunity to meet other researchers. On the one hand, archives, which are sometimes in isolated regions, can be lonely places. Moreover, the isolating, library-like nature of many archives prevents us from engaging in interactions with other researchers. And yet, during lengthy stays in the archives, I have made a conscious effort to meet and network with other historians. Consider your trip an opportunity to meet other researchers and build your network, but approach other researchers politely, paying attention to the fact that they have work to do, and consider your personality and comfort level when meeting new people.

If you have built a strong relationship with your archivist over the course of a lengthy stay, they also might help you to meet other researchers. This can happen in a number of ways. During my longest stay at an archive, I communicated my interests to the archivists who worked with me. I explained my dissertation project in depth as we moved along, and they eventually grew familiar with various components of the project. Later on, when I needed a break from my dissertation materials, I explained that I had a few ideas for future projects and the archivists helped me track down related materials to examine. Whenever another historian arrived at the archives with similar interests, the archivists I knew would send me an e-mail, saying something to the effect of, "Professor Stuart from Johns Hopkins will be at the archive on Tuesday, you might speak with him about the Miller Papers, which he examined during his last visit in 2007." When lunchtime rolled around on Tuesday, I might briefly introduce myself and invite Professor Stuart to lunch. While the vast majority of scholars are eager to talk about their work and learn about your projects, you should not expect everyone to be open to the idea of talking about their current research. Some scholars are guarded about their ideas and research, and it would be wise to respect that reticence. Some scholars might have scheduled every second of their visit to the archives and simply might not have the time to meet with you. Other scholars might be happy to find a willing audience to learn about their research and will offer you their thoughts on the state of the field and their own work.

7. Getting What You Came For

An ideal visit to the archives can feel a lot like the perfect day. You eat a healthy breakfast, have your trip to the archives well planned in advance, the archivists have your boxes ready when you arrive, and you find useful material to photograph from first folder to last. Maybe you even get to share lunch with another graduate student or faculty member in your field. Sadly, not all days at the archives will go exactly as planned. At the opposite extreme, it might be raining or snowing, the documents you get might turn out to be irrelevant, other researchers might have been rude and dismissive, and the archivist may have just noticed a dent on the side of his or her car, souring a normally cheerful mood. Typically, however, with strong preparation and a positive attitude, most archives provide historical researchers with a great experience and most archivists are sincerely interested in helping you find material relevant to your research. This section addresses some of the situations you may encounter in the archives and offers some suggestions for how to deal with them.

Restricted Materials

A restricted collection is a group of documents that are unavailable, or available only on a limited basis, to researchers. These restrictions are governed either by law or by a particular stipulation in the deed of gift that officially warranted the acquisition of the materials for the archive. Researchers should attempt to understand the factors behind the collection, preservation, and acquisition of the collections that they examine. In addition to the stipulations restricting personal collections, the federal government can restrict classified material until it is deemed no longer sensitive. Collections that are often restricted include information that could be deemed sensitive to identity theft, national security, or other legal and ethical issues. In a collection of personal papers, for example, an archive typically acquires the materials that the owner of the papers chose to donate. In addition to the ability to select which papers go into the collection, many archives will allow the donor of personal records to restrict or "seal" either all or parts of the collection. Often, these kinds of restrictions protect sensitive materials for a set period. A donor might request that his intimate love letters be restricted, preserved at the archive but kept from historical researchers, for a period of twenty-five years. The process of selecting which materials will be made available to historical researchers creates another layer of bias that historians should be aware of when conducting their research. Very often, researchers are surprised at the mundane nature of collections that donors choose to restrict. Further, archives prefer to make as much of their materials available as possible. Sometimes archives are obligated to compromise with donors, however, in order to obtain valuable collections.

Each archive will provide you with specific instructions for attempting to access restricted materials. If you do choose to file a request to view classified materials (often a Freedom of Information Act, or FOIA, request) follow the instructions carefully and be aware that the archival material might not become available to you for several months or even years.

Both public and private archives are typically bound by the terms of the Deed of Gift accompanying the donation of a particular collection. In the context of archives, a Deed of Gift is a legal document transferring ownership of source materials from private hands to the archive. Sometimes, the Deed of Gift will stipulate particular restrictions for the collection. This may include stipulations about the kinds of qualifications required for looking at certain collections or instructions for sealing documents from public view for a set number of years. An example of this kind of sensitive material might be a collection of personality tests conducted by a professional psychologist. If names were attached to each of the tests, this hypothetical collection might be restricted for a period of 100 years, until all participants in the study are almost certainly deceased. The archive may offer access to copies of the same tests with names blocked out. The legal documents accompanying the collection, or the so-called Deed of Gift, will detail these regulations. Periodically, archives will discuss and debate internally their desire for open access against their desire to obtain a particularly valuable collection. Archives will rarely collect and preserve collections that are to be permanently sealed, offering very limited or no access to researchers.

Historians should always consider the provenance of the historical documents they study. Where did this document come from? How did this collection arrive at the archive? Am I being given access to the entire collection or is a portion of this collection restricted or classified? How might these factors influence my understanding of the historical narrative? These are not easy questions to answer, but they are important to wrestle with in order to write a complex and well considered narrative. Often, the finding aids for specific collections detail how materials were acquired, and what kinds of materials are restricted. With some luck, archivists intimately familiar with particular collections, or archive staff who helped acquire a specific collection, will be willing to advise you on some of the many factors to consider when studying a collection in their archive.

LOST OR MISSING MATERIALS

Another reality of archives, museums, and libraries is that things get lost. Objects are stolen and sometimes placed on the black market. When reshelving items, an inexperienced intern or tired archivist can mistakenly place an object on the wrong shelf. These problems can cause issues for researchers or confuse future staff members who may try to find the object. I raise this point for two reasons. The first is that you should anticipate that some items will be lost or missing during the course of your research. A missing carton is not available for research, obviously. You are out of luck. When this happens, try to be understanding. Whatever you do, try not take out your frustration on the archivists you are working with. It is quite likely that they are in no way responsible for the fact the item has gone missing. The second point about missing objects and collections is that on certain occasions, your knowledge of an archive or particular collection might be helpful to the archivists you are working with. If you happen to spot a mistake or error in filing, perhaps one that might even confuse future reference archivists hoping to track down the material, simply point out the discrepancies and allow the concerned archivist to make any necessary corrections. Never try to refile or reorganize material on your own. Always allow the archivist to fix problems. Electronic access, especially in what we expect to be free and open societies, has the tendency to deceive us into believing that all printed material can be made available regularly and instantaneously. This is simply not true in the practical reality of caring for and keeping track of millions of rare objects. As a researcher, often the best thing to do is to alert the archive to the missing material (in the hope of it turning up later) before simply moving on to the next item on your list.

MATERIALS BEING PROCESSED

When an archive acquires new materials, a processing archivist is asked to organize and catalog the collection. As the archivist catalogs the new collection, they create a finding aid to guide future researchers. As a historian, understanding how archival collections are processed will help you in three ways. First, it is useful to understand how collections are acquired and organized in order to fully appreciate the context of the materials. Additionally, if you have a question related to a specific collection, a staff member of the archive may refer you to the "processing archivist." It is typically assumed that the archivist who organized and catalogd the collection will be the most knowledgeable. These archivists sometimes read through many, if not all, of the primary source documents in the collection and are sometimes asked to rearrange collections into a coherent system for future generations of archival staff and researchers, so they will have an intimate knowledge of the materials. Finally, you may be informed when you ask to see a newly acquired collection that the material is still being processed. This often means that the material is physically in the possession of the archive, but it has yet to be fully recorded, arranged, and catalogd. Different archives will have differing regulations about whether or not researchers can gain access to collections that are in the midst of being processed. A handful of archives will invite historians to view newly acquired collections to offer advice on how to organize the material, but most will not.

ENCOUNTERING THE UNEXPECTED

In an ideal world, a researcher in California can view an online finding aid for a well-organized collection in New York. The researcher can then travel to New York, fill out call slips at the archive or e-mail requests in advance, and the material that arrives at their desk in the archive will be exactly as described in the online finding aid. Unfortunately, this is not the way it always works. Sometimes researchers will find that archival materials described in finding aids or published secondary sources are quite different from what was expected. In a secondary source related to my research, the author reported that a watercolor artist illustrated a museum exhibition I was studying. From the description of the source, I expected to find copies of large paintings showing the entire course of the exhibition. Instead, I only found receipts for the purchase of the painting, the artist's brushes, and the canvas. It was only later in the collection that I discovered the watercolors were not actually portraits of the exhibit—they were simply color duplications of charts and graphs (watercolors served as a method of copying color graphs before there were color photographs or copiers). The description of the materials was technically accurate—watercolor reproductions had been made during the exhibition–they were just not what I expected. At the time, I had to remind myself that the error was in my expectations. In my mind, watercolor meant portraiture or landscape rather than graphs, so I had to learn a lesson from my disappointment.

As you are moving through archival sources and finding aids, it would be wise to recall that not all sources are exactly as described either online or in a finding aid. Spending the time to look at the sources in person will assure that you have an accurate idea of what the material actually looks like. All archival research is a careful balance between getting depth of material you need and making sure you find all the material that would benefit your research. Perhaps counter-intuitively, a number of historians actually recommend taking *fewer* notes and transcribing *less* to insure maximum coverage of materials in the collection. If you are successful in cutting down the amount of time you spend note taking, it might be possible to see a greater number of materials first hand. With any luck, some of the materials that appear to be only of marginal interest in the finding aid will turn out to be useful to your research. Take a moment to think over mistakes and unmet expectations when archival materials fail to correspond with their description, but move on to your next collection instead of dwelling on the problem. If a more accurate description might be added to the finding aid at the archive, you might suggest that to an archivist, but avoid getting bogged down away from your research.

8. Organizing Your Notes

Strong historical writing can be traced in part to effective note taking. Historians have to select from a wide array of different possible sources—ranging from secondary literature to a variety of archival collections—when creating a narrative. And unlike a finalized narrative, primary sources in the archives rarely have a clear beginning, middle, and end. Part of the goal in taking notes is to effectively and clearly organize primary source documents for later use in constructing a historical narrative.

Traditionally, historians organized their notes around a card system. Although your mentors may have discussed this system with you or you may have seen reference to it in older historical monographs, it is worth reiterating in this guide. Many historians used note cards to record valuable pieces of information gained from secondary readings or primary source materials. A quotation from a letter, for instance, could be written on the front, with citation information recorded on the back of the card. A historian could then organize the notes in any way he or she saw fit, arranging and rearranging the ideas gleaned from their sources in a different order and eventually creating an outline for a narrative. The quotations or ideas from each card could then be copied into a manuscript draft as it was created. Notes might include a brief transcription of the evidence and brief description of its significance to the overall argument or historical question. This system had several advantages. Note cards could be physically arranged and rearranged based on the project and your findings. Unlike writing in a notebook, a single note or small group of notes could easily be transferred from one point to another if doing so made sense. Note cards also helped historians think visually and were, in some sense, a physical manifestation of the historian's thoughts. They also likely contributed to the honing of the mental recall ability of generations of historians. Note cards, however, also possessed numerous disadvantages. They could easily be lost or misplaced. They lacked any sort of search function unless typed into a cumbersome database. They were time consuming to create. Finally, not all notes can be fitted onto a small card.

New note-taking systems, such as Zotero and Endnote, attempt to mimic older forms of note taking, while also making the notes both searchable and more compatible with the web (imagine writing down lengthy URLs on note cards!). However, a clear note taking system does not require a new piece of software. I have essentially replicated a series of note cards in my existing wordprocessing software, delineating a new document with a separate citation (for example, Letter to Robert Lowie from Franz Boas. December 16, 1924). Above that will be noted the folder and box numbers containing the primary source. While such a method can be useful, remember also to save a copy of these notes in the more permanent PDF format at the end of your visit. Later on, when you start to move these notes around as you construct a narrative, it can be easy to fail to transfer citation information if it is only listed at the top of a section of notes. Clearly define the contents of each source and note what words are original to the source, and what words are your own. I simply use quotation marks to highlight the original words, and bullet points with no quotation marks to indicate the significance of the document and where it fit into my broader claims.

Notes for your project can be based on themes, keywords, or individuals. My own notes are based on the archival collections themselves. I try to make my own collections of notes mirror the archival system, which, for me, makes for easy citations and easy recall. I keep my notes for manuscripts—where I organize and work through various ideas regarding my narrative—in a separate document. When taking notes on my laptop, I note at the top of each document the exact citation for the particular archival collection. Once I have created this document, I begin to read the archival material. Selecting which documents to transcribe or photographs to take is a skill I am constantly attempting to hone. As it might on occasion be difficult for me to return to some archives, I tend to err on the side of gathering even material that might seems only marginally relevant to my work—both in terms of gathering more archival materials and making bibliographic data as comprehensive as possible. Other historians recommend taking a more limited number of notes, as this will prevent you from becoming bogged down in your own materials later on. I typically ask myself how each document fits into my existing narrative arc or how it might change the manner in which I tell my basic story. Does it add detail, depth, or texture to the existing narrative? Is this collection of documents replicated somewhere else, or is it unique to this archive? If the document represents something valuable for my research, I transcribe it or photograph it, and record my actions that I have taken (noting, for example, where digital images of archival materials have been stored on my computer). I also transcribe or photograph documents that might be useful for lectures and discussion sections. A pamphlet or piece of ephemera advertising a world's fair, for instance, might make a nice slide for a lecture on international expositions. Although the document might not enhance the project I am currently working on, I try to reasonably determine what will be valuable later on without getting bogged down in tangential work.

When transcribing a document, you should ask yourself if the notes you have taken will make sense several weeks or months later, when you are mentally and physically removed from the collection. To ensure that my notes will continue to make sense, I sometimes include an introductory sentence or two above the document recording my notes. The introductory sentence is not marked with quotation marks, so I know the sentences are in my own language. Generally, this short introductory statement simply summarizes my thoughts on how this collection might relate to the overall project. These thoughts might be based partially on clues provided by the finding aid or a conversation with an archivist. Later on, when transcribing a document from a collection, a letter might be introduced with a brief sentence or two explaining that the previous set of letters revolved around a philosophical argument that this letter continued to address. You might suspect that a particular individual was the author of an anonymous memorandum, or speculate from other evidence that an undated document was created at a specific time. Your introductory notes to that document could simply remind you of your initial suspicion. If you are lucky, collections of documents will reveal to you a basic story that you are hoping to tell in your narrative. Remind yourself throughout your notes of the pieces of a story as it comes together.

ORGANIZING DIGITAL FILES

A lengthy day in the archives can result in dozens or even hundreds of photographs or scans, in addition to transcribed notes. If you are taking or transferring notes to your computer, there is the potential to lose valuable information or misplace the correct citation for the documents. How do you keep all of those files organized? Just as with basic note-taking systems, researchers will have to develop a system for organizing files based on their own research projects and habits.

My own digital files are broken down into two basic components. When I arrive at a new archive, I create a new electronic folder labeled with the name of the archive. If I am, for example, looking at three separate collections on the day that I visit a new archive, within the folder I have created for the large archive, I create three separate folders for each particular collection I am planning to explore. Within the collection folders, I start a new document in a word processing program to record the photographs I have taken or to transcribe and describe written documents. When photographing, I take pictures of the outside labels of boxes, folder labels, and the documents themselves. Then, on the master document for the collection I record what photographs have been taken and assign a citation to particular documents. The advantage of this system is that I can look back at my notes several weeks or months later and be reminded of exactly where a collection of transcribed documents or photographs was originally found and provide a complete citation for the collection. The disadvantage, however, is that I need to recall what collection a document was in to track it down (applications such as Google Desktop and Windows Search can help streamline this process). While this system works well for me, others may find it confusing if they are working with numerous collections with overlapping names and keywords. Each historian should develop a unique system based around their strengths for memory and recall as well as one geared to their particular kinds of archival materials.

Organizing Physical Files

As a historical researcher, you will likely acquire a number of photocopies of original archival documents as well as a collection of permission forms and paperwork from archives. As you begin your work in the archives, consider how best to store these types of files. Will they go in your filing cabinet? Will you choose to digitize them? Early on in my career, I made a large number of photocopies of original documents. Over the past few years, I have transitioned away from photocopies toward digital photographs, scans, and transcriptions made on my computer. Nevertheless, some paper documents are simply unavoidable. As you begin your work, consider how these types of documents will be stored alongside your growing personal archive. Once again, I organize these files by archive. If you are making a large number of photocopies, however, you should consider creating an organizational system that is more specific to your subject—chronologically or thematically, for instance—and meets the needs of your work.

9. Conclusion

This pamphlet is meant to be a helpfully practical guide to conducting historical research in the archives. But every archive, big or small, has its own ways of facilitating research, whether in terms of the kinds of catalogs it maintains, the finding aids it provides, or in the rules it imposes on the access to, and use of, its materials. In a sense, therefore, even after consulting such informative resources as the Archives Wiki of the American Historical Association (archiveswiki.historians.org) or the web sites of specific archives, every visit to an archive will be a fascinating voyage into an uncharted territory. But that is, as every researcher learns, part of the excitement of exploring an archive: the serendipitous discovery or the intriguing threads of detection that you can often follow till you can weave a more complete picture of the particular slice of the past that is your subject. This brief guide is an attempt to help make that exploration a little easier, and a little more productive.

10. Some Quick Tips

◆ **Explore before you go**. Study the web site of the archive in advance and try to figure out which collections you will be examining. Then, take some time to familiarize yourself with the finding aids for these collections online. Plug relevant keywords into the online catalog provided by the archive or library if they have one available on the web. This will not only be helpful in navigating the collections, but will also provide you with the appropriate background to maximize the time spent with archivists. Don't be surprised if the actual archives differ wildly from the information listed on the web site. Nevertheless, scoping out the information they have posted on the web is always a good idea.

◆ **Write ahead.** Always check ahead to make sure the archive will be open when you arrive, and the materials you need will be available when you get there. Schedule an appointment and provide archivists or research assistants with an idea of what you are hoping to examine during your stay. Some archives will not allow visits from unqualified research-ers or scholars who fail to make an appointment. Other archives have a limited number of seats to offer to research-ers each day. Additionally, when contacting the archives early, make sure to describe your general interests as they may have a specialist who covers those topics.

◆ **Bring a sweater.** When working in muggy Washing-ton or Atlanta it might be hard to convince yourself to pack a sweater, but after a couple of hours in a heavily air-conditioned building you'll be happy you brought one! Remember that archives and libraries have a responsibility to preserve documents, and papers and often have tightly regulated, cool temperatures. Don't forget that some archives do not allow zip-up sweaters or hooded sweatshirts. Archives typically reserve the right to determine what is considered "outerwear."

◆ **Follow the rules.** Archives possess widely divergent rules and regulations for researchers. Review the rules listed on their web site before you leave home, and listen carefully to the archivist's instructions when you get there. They will likely have a different procedure for your coat, bag, papers, and technology use from the last archive where you worked. Some archives are stricter than others; it is to your advantage to follow the rules as they are explained to you. Most archives prominently list many regulations throughout the research area, so refer back to these postings regularly until you are thoroughly familiar with the protocol.

◆ **Treat the archive as though you are a guest.**

◆ **Remember archivists are professionals too.** Many of them have specialized training and hold graduate degrees. Treat them as colleagues. Most of these individuals will know the collection far better than you, so use them as a resource!

◆ **Carefully record what you find in the archive.** You'll be grateful eight months later when you're trying to reconstruct the narrative that you've discovered in the archives. Even if you don't think a document is useful now, remember that it may be useful later—attempt make a basic record of everything you see.

◆ **Develop an organizational strategy.** More information is better: you will not remember as much as you think you will. Most historians develop their organization system through trial and error. If possible, develop your archival method through practice on smaller projects. Consider writing a brief article, for example, or discussing organizational strategies with other scholars.

◆ **Take notes on all that you find.** Just as important as recording information about useful sources is recording which sources are not useful. This will help you avoid having to retrace your steps through documents not worth your time.

Some researchers write a daily log summarizing what they've accomplished in the archives. This serves as a good reference point when returning to the archives, offers the opportunity to reflect on the day's findings, and creates a tangible "end-of-day" that can be useful.

◆ **Anticipate some disappointment:** Not every collection in the archive will be organized. Sometimes it is not even open or available to researchers. Recognize that the archivists are often involved in a number of different projects at once, and do not expect any archival staff to drop everything to process a particular collection for you. This is not only presumptuous, but also unrealistic: many collections require hundreds of man-hours before being considered a fully processed collection.

◆ **Get organized.** You may find many documents about the same incident in a number of different places; they may be categorized in the archives by name, date, place, or person. Think in advance about how you will organize potentially divergent collections about the same topic. And once you leave the archives, reorganize your notes while the material is still fresh in your mind. Also, take the time to organize and file away your photographs, scans, or photocopies.

◆ **Know what you are looking for.** One archivist passed along a memorable quote from a researcher who liked to ask, "Who gets the right answers?" The response—"The people who ask the right questions." The quote, the archivist explained to me, related to how historical researchers approach archives. If you are able to explain your research questions in the clear terms, an archivist will likely be able to help you.

◆ **Know how to get the information you need.** Ask the archivist how they would like you to "mark" or "flag" documents. Documents can be marked for photocopies, as you pull them from the box, or if you desire to come back to them later. Most archives will provide researchers with "acid-free" or "archivally sound" slips of paper to hold a particular place in an archival collection.

◆ **Practice your "elevator talk."** Work on a brief explanation of your overall project, describing in a few sentences each portion of the larger project. You can practice giving this summary presentation orally. Similarly, be prepared to ask a few questions of your fellow researchers about the projects they are working on. If you have business cards, make sure to bring them to the archive.

◆ **Show your true colors.** If you feel comfortable doing so, periodically wear a t-shirt, or sweatshirt with the name or logo of your school on it. It can be a conversation starter with fellow alums who spot you in the reading room. Remember that some archives will not allow hats or zip sweatshirts, so be sure to check the rules of the archive as you pack.

◆ **Start a file listing the people you meet.** Don't be so committed to your work that you stop socially interacting with people. It is likely that you only have so much time in the archives. That time is precious. Nevertheless, a quick conversation with another researcher in the archives can go a very long way in assisting your career. This file can include a list of the faculty you've met on your home campus as well as the archivists and researchers you meet in the archives. Include contact information, a brief description of their position or research interests, and any other information that you think might be useful. A business card, if you have one, can come in handy for exchanging contact information.

◆ **Learn about local research tools.** Many large archives, or small archives embedded within much larger institutions, possess their own, unique, tools for finding what you need within archival collections. Explore the web site for the archive and ask around to discover the best way to search the collection. Once you have been referred to a particular web site or database, do your best to master it before your trip to the archives. The more time you are able to spend with these tools before you actually arrive at the archive, the more time you will save for actual work with documents.

11. Definitions of Terms

Researchers should familiarize themselves with some of the terms routinely used in archives. Learning to "speak the language" of the archives takes a little time, but will benefit you as a researcher because a shared vocabulary helps to communicate your requirements and needs more quickly and clearly to the staff of the archives.

◆ **Accession**—Museums, libraries, and archives often use the term "accession" to define a grouping of acquired materials. For instance, if personal papers are donated by the next of kin following a death, an archive would group the materials as an "accession." If, years later, a distant relative of the same person donates another collection of related papers, the material would be grouped with the original archival documents, but this collection would be tracked as a separate accession.

◆ **Acid-Free Paper**—Acid-free paper possesses a neutral PH level and does not contain the chemicals in most paper that expel gases over time, damaging archival materials.

◆ **Archive**—The word archive can mean either a collection of records or the physical location where records are stored. An archive is an institution that holds and cares for primary source materials. Those who require primary source materials for research—historians, journalists, lawyers, indigenous peoples, and students, for instance—frequently utilize archives to reconstruct the past. Archives are often established as part of a larger institution, but some archives are independent nonprofit organizations or are associated with particular businesses.

◆ **Archival Material**—For historians, this term usually means the primary source material that they find in archives. For archivists, however, the term connotes material that is considered to be "archivally sound." That is, material that is paper, cardboard, or plastic that will not harm primary source documents they contain. Non-archival paper, cardboard, and plastics slowly leach oils, gases, and vapors that can be harmful to fragile documents.

◆ **Call Slip**—A call slip is a document used to request materials from the archive. Most call slips require the following information: your name, date, collection title and box numbers. Typically, call slips will have spaces to easily record the information you have found in the finding aid. Once transferred to the reference archivist the call slip will be used to find your requested materials in storage. Call slips are also known as "out cards." Paper call slips are gradually being replaced at many archives by electronic call slips (usually simple web forms mirroring the older paper slips). Call slips usually feature space for researchers to indicate call numbers, titles, and author names; but each archive will have its own specific requirements. You may also be asked to indicate a researcher number or a seat in the reading room of the archive so that your request can be properly tracked and fulfilled.

◆ **Catalog**—A systematically arranged list and description of material in an archive. Archivists, just as librarians, have historically utilized card catalog systems - simple paper index cards to organize discreet objects in a collection. Modern archives catalog collections in a variety of formats from paper binders, to microfiche, to easily accessible digital databases. Most archival catalogs found online are now keyword searchable and many also feature digitized collections.

◆ **Catalog Record**—Each particular "catalog record" describes the archival material. Typically, catalog records detail the size of the collection (often in "linear feet") and explain the scope of the materials and the kinds of documents found within the collection (correspondence, photographs, prints, etc.).

◆ **Conservation**—Conservation is the process of preserving, caring for, and repairing original materials. The practitioners of conservation—or "conservators" vary in expertise, specializing in paper, paintings, photographs or objects. Many smaller archives will outsource the conservation of collections to larger institutions or nonprofit conservation organizations. Conservators generally have a strong background in both science and the field in which they are conserving materials. There is a difference between conservation and restoration of archival material. Most conservators only perform repairs that can easily be undone while restoration tends to be more permanent. Conservators can, in fact, repair items, but their goal is not to restore a document to its original appearance – rather to ensure its ongoing preservation.

◆ **Copyright**—Copyright refers to the ownership of a series of rights related to a particular document or photograph. Most commonly, issues of copyright revolve around legal permissions in publishing or reproducing specific documents. When preparing to publish a manuscript with quotations or reproductions of photographs, historical researchers should always write to the appropriate archive for permission to publish. See also "Permissions."

◆ **Deed of Gift**—A Deed of Gift is a legal agreement accompanying a donation to a particular institution. For archival collections, the Deed of Gift will often transfer ownership of the collection, but can also contain a number of different kinds of restrictions. Access to archival collections can be restricted to qualified researchers or sealed for a set number of years. Generally, an archive will have the Deed of Gift on file and can inform you of any particular restrictions surrounding the collection.

◆ **Finding Aid**—A finding aid is a document of varying length and complexity describing an archival collection. Most finding aids contain the following sections: biographical note, bibliography, processing note, and collection inventory. The collection inventory is the most useful portion of the finding aid, and identifies box numbers and folder titles. This reference tool can help you locate particular kinds of documents within a larger collection. Whereas a catalog entry will list basic information about a specific collection, a finding aid will offer a more detailed explanation of the contents within the collection. A finding aid, for example, might list the exact box numbers of specific correspondents, whereas the catalog entry might only list the names of correspondents in the collection, or simply that the collection contains correspondence.

♦ **Institutional Records**—Institutional records are the archival materials related to a particular organization. Like personal papers, they can include letters, memoranda, and photographs, but the records typically relate to the operations of the institution. Just as with personal papers, they can be organized thematically, chronologically, or by creator. Some organizations such as corporations, museums, or universities have regulations that govern the intellectual property rights in the records created during the operation of an institution. Letters written by a museum curator and related to the business of the institution, for example, may become the property of the museum, rather than the curator, upon his or her retirement.

♦ **Light Box**—A light box is a device that provides light for viewing photographic documents, including slides, glass plates and photographic negatives. Light boxes that are appropriate for use in the archives avoid giving off too much heat in order to prevent damage to the documents. Almost always, light boxes are provided by the archive. A light box usually has a base on which the documents being viewed can be placed.

♦ **Linear Foot**—A unit used by archivists to describe the size of an archive. A "linear foot" of documents implies the total number of archival material that could be shelved in approximately 12 inches of shelf space. Typically, each linear foot comprises a couple of average-size archival boxes. Finding aids will generally provide information on the size of collections or record groups in terms of linear feet. Some archival material will be arranged by cubic foot rather than linear foot. Expect to spend, at the very least, a day for every 10 linear feet of material.

◆ **Microform (Microfilm/Microfiche)**—Microform is a term used to describe document reproduction systems based on film. These systems come in a variety of formats, all of which benefit archives by providing additional copies of materials— offering the advantage of not harming the originals through normal wear during research—and saving space. Microform copies are sometimes used to reproduce personal papers or institutional records, but they are perhaps most commonly associated with newspaper records. Microfilm reproductions are placed on reels which can be viewed in a microfilm reader. Microfiche also reproduces paper records, but these are on flat cards instead of reels. Both kinds of microform require a machine to read. The archive will usually provide the appropriate reading machines.

◆ **Original Order**—Original order refers to the scheme for organizing materials utilized by the creator. The original order for a collection will provide intellectual context for the collection. Many archivists will argue that regardless of whether the original order of a collection makes coherent sense otherwise, this scheme should be maintained to best preserve the context for the collection. Archivists will attempt to preserve—to the extent possible—the original order of a donor's documents unless the collection arrives at the archive with no coherent order, thus requiring the archive to impose an intellectually coherent scheme for organizing the collection. A good finding aid will note in the introductory or processing note if the original order of a collection was altered and to what extent materials have been rearranged by the archive.

◆ **Permissions**—(see also "copyright")—Due to a variety of copyright issues and the legal contracts surrounding particular donations, historical researchers hoping to publish archival information in any format (quotations in manuscripts or photographs on web sites, for example) should check with the archive regarding their policies regarding permissions. These policies range from forms documenting each archival quotation to be used in particular publications to simple e-mail agreements.

◆ **Personal Papers**—Personal papers are the letters, memoranda, photographs, and diaries of particular individuals stored in an archive. Sometimes referred to as "private papers."

◆ **Preservation Copy**—If original documents are too fragile to be used for creating copies, a master copy of the original document might be set aside to use for future reproductions. The original copy, then, is typically not used for research unless absolutely necessary.

◆ **Primary Source**—An original document or source of information from the period of interest to the historical researcher. Primary sources include letters, maps, photographs, and oral histories. Archives are typically repositories of collections of primary sources.

◆ **Processing**—Archivists use the term "processing" to describe the description and arrangement of a collection of primary sources. Processing a collection usually results in the organization of the collection as well as the creation of a finding aid to help researchers navigate the collection. Depending on the nature of the archive (the available funding and staff) and the size and sophistication of the new collection, processing material can take anywhere from a few days to several years. Processing can involve appraisal, arrangement, description, and preservation.

◆ **Provenance**—Provenance as it relates to archival collections is the determination of the context of the creation of a collection. Archivists ask where and how a collection was created to better understand what it represents intellectually. Many archivists consider the provenance and the original order of a collection when organizing documents, working to best preserve the order in which the documents were created or, if necessary, impose a coherent and logical order upon the collection. See also "Original Order."

◆ **Pull Time**—Some larger archives utilize a system to minimize or streamline requests for documents from researchers. Archives within the National Archives system, including many, but not all of the presidential libraries, operate under a pull-time system. This system dictates when you are able to request archival material from storage. When estimating time that has to be spent at a particular archives, it will be necessary to allow for the time-lags imposed by the pull-time system (if it is being implemented by the archives).

◆ **Reading Room**—The reading room is the primary location where historical researchers can view archival documents. Each reading room has particular rules that will usually be explained to the researcher when first entering the space.

◆ **Reference Archivist**—An archivist whose primary role is to assist researchers in the archive. Reference archivists often have backgrounds in the subject matter of the archives (history, anthropology, science, and so forth) and they often have advanced degrees in information and library sciences.

◆ **Repository**—This term is sometimes used as a synonym for "archives." Traditionally, the term repository identifies a storehouse for primary source material including manuscripts and documents. This term is also used for rare book libraries, historical societies, and buildings holding government and institutional records.

◆ **Restricted collections**—Restricted collections are primary source materials that have been classified or otherwise designated unavailable to historical researchers. Restrictions can be imposed by donors or mandated by the archive. Materials commonly restricted include: medical records, psychological tests, student records, personnel files, classified government documents etc. Some documents may be restricted for a set amount of time. Examples of this kind include sensitive government documents or personal letters between a husband and wife that might be temporarily restricted until the death of the living spouse.

For more terms or expanded definitions, see "A Glossary of Archival and Records Terminology" on the Society for American Archivists webpage (http://www.archivists.org/glossary).

APPENDIX A
READING AND ARCHIVING
ORAL HISTORIES

Library-based oral history programs—such as those at Columbia University and the University of California, Berkeley—have long treated oral histories as functionally equivalent to other kinds of archival materials such as manuscripts, letters, maps, rare books, or diaries. Modern practitioners of oral history, however, are driven more by research frameworks than models for collecting. Modern historians bring to bear more diverse and interdisciplinary methods for critical readings of texts. Even as methods for reading and interpreting oral histories have shifted, a tradition of collecting transcribed oral history interviews—as well as original audio and video material—can be found in archives both in the United States and abroad. To successfully read, interpret, and use oral history texts (whether they are transcripts or original recordings), they must be read critically, in a fashion analogous to other kinds of historical source material. Additionally, the researcher will find it helpful to think like an oral historian—consider the questions that are asked, the primary themes of the interview, life-stage of the narrator in terms of the role of retrospection in narration, and the shared or contrasting goals of the interviewer and narrator. Some readers of oral history texts utilize theory in areas such as memory, narrative, orality, performance, intersubjectivity, and power. The exact approach taken to these problems depends on the research project and the methods chosen by the researcher, but you should always consider the many complex dynamics at play in the course of the creation of oral history sources.

Oral histories are archived in many formats—original audio, video, and sometimes, but not always, complete transcripts with abstracts, author introductions, and descriptive tables of contents. All types of historical sources—ranging from illuminated manuscripts to maps, diaries, and oral histories—need to be read using a critical framework common across many methods of practicing history. As historians, we question authorial voice of all documents, critically examine the historical context surrounding each document, and attempt to utilize particular documents in our own arguments and narrative frames. That is, historians explore primary sources to better understand their own developing narratives about change over time. Accessing and recording the memories of individuals with first-hand experiences related to particular events, communities, and organizations can work to support *or* upend arguments put forward by scholars using more traditional sources. Human memory, however, is both fallible and malleable. Oral histories, should, therefore be read carefully and critically in the light of evidence from other available sources. You should, of course, read *all* your sources with attention to detail and a critical eye. Working with oral history sources also requires you to ask a series of questions unique to the source materials—including transcripts, audio, and sometimes, video. For example, when working with a transcript, check the written text against the original audio file when possible in order to understand the nature of the editing, the meaning of pauses, accents, silences, and expressions of emotion. If video is available, consider the visual information about the narrator that is communicated. Historians and archivists generally consider the original audio or video document to be the original primary source material produced by an oral history interview; however, important details can be added to the transcript by either the interviewer or narrator. Ideally, serious researchers will have an opportunity to critically read the transcript *and* listen to the original recordings.

Here are some points to consider when embarking on a project that involves conducting your own oral history interviews:

◆ Consider enrolling in a training course or workshop. Traditionally, these have been offered by a variety of organizations. The oral history offices of the University of California, Berkeley, Columbia University, and Baylor University are just three of many examples.

◆ Abide by the ethical and protocol guidelines laid out by Human Subjects Review Committees (IRB) and the Oral History Association (OHA). In fact, if you are affiliated with a university or college in the United States, you should consider the IRB committee on your campus as a resource for working with people in your research. The protocols often include specific approaches and formats for confidentiality agreements, consent forms, and legal releases that may be necessary for your project.

◆   Consider how your materials will be archived for future use by historians. Once your project is complete, I encourage you to make your oral histories as accessible as possible through a reputable archive such as a nearby university or historical society. Unless the narrator (or person being interviewed) has requested that material be sealed or material remain unpublished you should encourage the use of your oral histories by other researchers and teachers by making them accessible online, in an archive, or preferably *both*. Consider also donating your notes or materials that provide further context for future scholars.

Assess oral history sources critically:

◆   Who conducted the oral history? What are the potential biases?

◆   How heavily has the oral history transcript been edited? How accurate is it in faithfully transcribing the original audio (and video)?

◆   What were the motivations of the narrators (or interviewees)? How are their memories and recollections colored by personal perspectives, political beliefs, or their particular gender, religion, sexual orientation, etc.? How might have race, gender, age, religion, and sexual orientation affected or influenced the nature of the interview? Were any power dynamics at play that shaped the interview?

◆   What was the purpose of a particular oral history? Was the conversation driven by a specific research project? Was the focus of the interview the subject's relationship to a particular institution (the University History Series of the Regional Oral History Office at the University of California, Berkeley; or the Smithsonian Institution's Oral and Videohistory collections within the Institutional History Division, for example) or a geographic region (such as University of North Carolina's Southern Oral History Program)?

◆　If you're reading a transcribed version of the oral history, are original audio and video materials available in the archive? These original materials can provide special insights not available in the transcript. When possible, serious researchers should listen to the original audio and video while they review the transcript.

◆　As a historian, consider what has been said—and hasn't been said—in the interview, as well as providing a thoughtful consideration of the questions that have not been addressed in the oral history. Reading and listening for silences can be as illuminating as what is actually said in an oral history interview.

Yes, oral history sources pose many challenges. But read with care and a from a critical perspective, the diligent historian will often discover in oral history texts a history that is a nuanced and revealing source when compared to traditional records found in archives.

APPENDIX B:
READING A PRIMARY SOURCE
DOCUMENT

Primary sources are documents, images, or objects, which originate from the period under research. Historians read primary sources with a critical eye before utilizing them as key pieces of evidence buttressing their narratives. Frequently, historians refer to and enter into conversation with primary source material in supporting arguments.

Although not all primary sources are housed in archives, archival repositories in the United States and around the world serve a critical function in preserving, cataloging, and providing access to countless (often irreplaceable) documents that provide us with a richer and more complete understanding of the past. As you work through archival records, consider carefully how you as a researcher are reading, interpreting, and utilizing these sources. Consider too, that archives—like museums and libraries—collect material based on individual determinations of significance. In other words, every archive considers which materials are important enough to collect and preserve based on the mission of the archive.

When thinking historically, researchers attempt to contextualize primary and secondary sources, developing works of historical imagination drawn from available evidence. Historians contextualize sources by explaining the relevant social, cultural, political, and environmental factors contributing to change over time. Modern day historians borrow techniques from a broad array of humanistic disciplines; theorists from the likes of anthropology, sociology, psychology, law, and literary criticism can provide you with key tools for interpreting the primary sources you discover. Here are some guiding questions that will help you learn to interrogate primary sources.

Ask key questions of all sources:

◆ Who authored the text? What can you find out about this author?

◆ What are the goals and aims of this document? Why was it written? Did the author have specific motivations?

◆ Is the source credible? Why or why not?

◆ What other sources can I find to support or corroborate this source?

◆ Does this document support the arguments made by other historians or does it work to refute previous claims?

◆ What was the audience for this source? How many people read the source in the time you are researching?

◆ How did this document end up in the archive, can the history its of acquisition and preservation help you understand the source?

In the case of images:

◆ Who created the image? What was the purpose of creating the image?

◆ What motivated the image-maker?

◆ How has the image been altered through various stages of reproduction and printing?

In the case of films:

◆ If there are people in the film, what are they doing?

◆ Was the film intended as an accurate non-fictional representation of reality or does it claim to be fictional on some level?

◆ What environment is depicted?

◆ How is technology used by the filmmaker? Consider the camera, lens, film, level of production, etc.

◆ Has the film been modified from its original? If so, how?

In the case of written documents:

- If the document provides an argument (or has a thesis) can you summarize it?

- What are the most important words in the document?

- What keywords can be further researched?

In the case of audio recordings such as oral history:

- What are the speakers saying? Do they have personal experiences related to an event, person, or thing under study?

- Consider not only the words being spoken but also the ambient, surrounding noise, or the "soundscape"—such as crying children, trains, sirens, or music. What can these sounds tell you about the recording?

- Silences too can be meaningful and powerful—they can indicate a surprising (yet often tangled) array of emotions or ideas.

Finally, ask yourself several key questions about being a reader:

- Why am I reading this source?

- Does this source support my argument?

If alternative arguments might have been made, what are they? Why did I reject these interpretations? What other lines of reasoning might have been followed?

Notes

1. The most basic book on archives management is Jeanette White Ford, *Archival Principles and Practice: A Guide for Archives Management* (Jefferson, N.C.: McFarland & Co., 1990). Although this volume is intended to be a beginner's guide to the subject of archives, it contains valuable information and useful definitions of terms for students of history and archives.

2. Ford, *Archival Principles and Practice*, 26.

3. See the discussion of this in Jeanette White Ford, *Archival Principles and Practice: A Guide for Archives Management* (Jefferson, N.C.: McFarland & Co., 1990), 29–33.